GROW YOURSELF SUCCESSFUL

PAULA PALMER GREEN

Pea Green Publishing

Grow Yourself Successful

Copyright © 2011 by Paula Palmer Green

Cover Design & Page Layout by suka.dsain@gmail.com

ISBN: 978-0-615-54194-5

Published by

Pea Green Publishing

Atlanta, GA 30344

All rights reserved under International Copyright Law. Contents may not be reproduced in whole or part in any form without expressed written consent from the publisher.

Printed in the United States of America

DEDICATION

This book is dedicated to You

for having the courage

to be who you want to be,

to do what you want to do

and to have what you want to have.

ACKNOWLEDGEMENTS

First and foremost, I thank God for forming, filling and guiding me to complete this book. Mama, thank you for pushing me to my purpose and loving me unconditionally. Billie I'm greener because of your love. Grant you are my emerald and more. Billie II, Vick and Miy thanks for helping me to grow stronger. Paulette, thanks for keeping me focused and being a great big sister. Dr. Belinda Davis Smith, having you as my sister friend makes the journey happier. Dr. Maude, Diana and Sheila O. your encouragement and support were immeasurable. Natasha, Mallorie, and Mr. David et al – you rock. Dr. Kiehle, thanks for believing in me and helping me write right. Brett Bell, you're the man! *Monanificent you make me want to be excellent*. Ellena your insight was and is empowering. Bishop Bronner, Dr. Nina and my WOF family, thanks for keeping me spiritually grounded for earthly good.

CONTENTS

DEDICATION		3
ACKNOWLEDGEMENTS		5
INTRODUCTION		9
CHAPTER 1	:Make Your Mark	13
CHAPTER 2	:Embracing Your Potential	19
CHAPTER 3	:The Dash	27
CHAPTER 4	:Heart vs. Head	35
CHAPTER 5	:Seeing the Invisible	39
CHAPTER 6	:Being a Gift	43
CHAPTER 7	:Brand Yourself	47
CHAPTER 8	:Looking the Part	55
CHAPTER 9	:Heed & Heard	63
CHAPTER 10	:Your Words – Your World	71
CHAPTER 11	:Encourage Others and Empower Yourself	79
CHAPTER 12	:Living More Fully	87
CHAPTER 13	:Making it Work Together	93
EPILOGUE		95

INTRODUCTION

Your idea of success is totally different from someone else's. It is different because you are different. You are unique with your own thoughts, talents and desires just to name a few. You were made for a certain purpose. There is something that you do extremely well. It comes naturally to you. You really don't have to put forth any effort to do it. And when you do it – you come alive. Your adrenalin flows; there is a smile on your face and contentment in your heart.

You might take what you do extremely well for granted. Please know that what comes naturally to you doesn't come naturally to someone else. Your challenge is to claim what it is that you do well, figure out a way to do it as much as possible and get paid for doing it.

It doesn't matter where you are in your life. You might be working on a job and or pursuing an occupation that you abhor or you might need a job. First off, be thankful for your job. In today's economy – having a job is a true blessing. Know that your job takes up only about 8 hours of your 24 hour day. You still have time to pursue the things that you like to do.

And in so doing, you will position yourself for greater success by simply embracing a higher calling which is your vocation.

As a child you attended school to learn how to learn and to learn how to make a living. If you always knew what you wanted to be when you grew up – I applaud you. You are more than likely doing what you love to do and getting paid to do so. But if you found out late about your true talent or if you are stuck in an unsatisfying job, position or predicament – this book will help you identify, articulate and market your special gift.

You will be introduced to tried and tested techniques to put you on track to do more of what you love to do.

If you are looking for inspiration, motivation and answers to help you be more successful, join me as we *Grow Yourself Successful!*

"Success means having the courage, the determination, and the will to become the person you believe you were meant to be."

GEORGE SHEEHEN

CHAPTER

MAKE YOUR MARK

"Every man and woman is born into the world to do some thing unique and something distinctive and if he or she does not do it, it will never be done."

– Benjamin E. Mays

How well do you know what you were born to do? If you are not sure, just ask the people who love you the most. Beyond a shadow of a doubt, they will tell you without hesitation. While you are at it – don't settle for one person's opinion, ask several people.

The feedback that you receive will be similar in nature. Your challenge is to find, own and do that which you were made to do. Once you begin to do what you were made to do – your life will take on a whole new meaning.

Sometimes we experience inner conflict when we fail to find, follow and bring to the forefront of our lives the thing that we were born to do which in essence is our life's purpose. When we embrace our purpose for being here, we begin to live life more fully. And we position ourselves to leave a lasting legacy.

Join me as we work towards you making a mark on the earth that cannot be erased.

EXERCISE – MY LIFE LINE

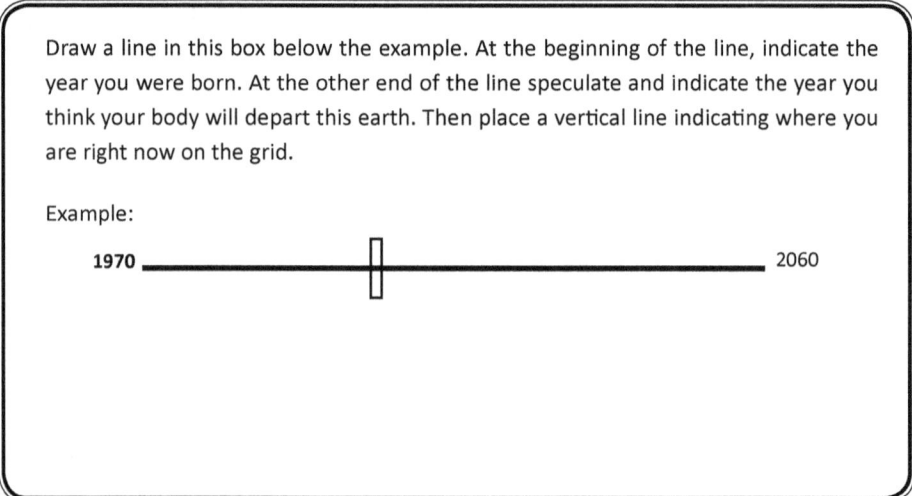

This life line exercise is a wonderful way for you to see just how much time you think you have left on this earth. What happened prior to the mark where you think you are is irrelevant. You cannot change the past.

What you have experienced in your life thus far contributes to the person you are today. A prayer that is near and dear to my heart is called The Serenity Prayer. I had to remember it in the 5th grade. The words did not mean that much to me at the time. But over the years I have reflected on their meaning and relevance to my life.

THE SERENITY PRAYER

God grant me the serenity
to accept the things I cannot change;
courage to change the things I can;
and wisdom to know the difference.

You cannot change who your parents are or were, where you were born, your height, your race, and certain things that happened to you thus far. You can change, to name a few: your weight, class, intellect, appearance, etc.

EXERCISE – MY PERSONAL CHANGE LIST

List three things that you would like to change about yourself:

1. ....
2. ....
3. ....

Practically every book that you could ever read on the subject of personal development will advise you to put your desires in writing. One thing I know for sure is that if you put what you want in writing – you have a better chance of seeing it come to fruition.

The way we record and receive information is rapidly changing. Computers are replacing books and paper. To that end, you decide how you want to capture your desires. Type, text or write them - just make sure you can hold them in your hand on a sheet of paper.

It is said that we become what we behold. To see your desires fulfilled, why not behold them? Write them out, or print them out on paper to keep you focused on whatever it is you want to see materialize. Some people place their list of desires with deadlines on their mirrors, in their cars, Bibles, wallets you name it.

Take a look at the next exercise. Jot down what you need to do to change the three things that you want to change about yourself. You will notice that there is a box at the bottom of each desire. The box is for you to identify a date by which you want the change to occur. Under each of the three changes, list actions you will take to manifest your desired goal.

If I asked you if you could eat an elephant, what would you say? Granted you cannot put an elephant in your mouth at one time. But you can eat away at it one bite at a time. The same principle applies to attaining your goal. Everyday do a little something to help you reach your goal on or before your anticipated goal completion date.

> *"You must take personal responsibility.*
> *You cannot change the circumstances,*
> *the seasons, or the wind, but you can*
> *change yourself."*
>
> JIM ROHN

EXERCISE – MY PERSONAL CHANGE IMPLEMENTATION LIST

Change I :_____
Action

_____ (Anticipated Completion Date:)

Change II :_____
Action

_____ (Anticipated Completion Date:)

Change III :_____
Action

_____ (Anticipated Completion Date:)

How bad do you want to be more successful? Please know that you must be willing to change in order to be more successful. Congratulations on identifying what you need to change in order to grow. Make a copy of your Personal Change Implementation List. Display your copy where you can see it daily and remember to do something everyday towards reaching your completion dates.

"Those who are victorious plan effectively
and change decisively.
They are like a great river that maintains its course
but adjusts its flow."

SUN TZU

CHAPTER

EMBRACING YOUR POTENTIAL

Those who improve with age embrace the power of personal growth and personal achievement and begin to replace youth with wisdom, innocence with understanding and lack of purpose with self-actualization."

— Bo Bennett

What do you need to be more successful? To truly understand human needs, we can look to Psychologist Abraham Maslow. Maslow[1] presents a hierarchy of needs pyramid which can be divided into basic (or deficiency) needs (i.e. physiological, safety, love, and esteem) and growth needs (cognitive, aesthetics and self-actualization). One must satisfy lower level basic needs before progressing on to meet higher level growth needs. Once these needs have been reasonably satisfied, one may be able to reach the highest level called self-actualization.

Take a moment to study this pyramid and complete the following exercise to identify what you need at this point and time in your life.

SELF-ACTUALIZATION
(Achieving Individual Potential)

ESTEEM
(Self-esteem and Esteem from Others)

BELONGING
(Love, affection, being a part Groups)

SAFETY
(Shelter, removal from danger)

PHYSIOLOGICAL
(Health, food, sleep)

EXERCISE – MY NEED

> I need the following to achieve my potential

Now that you have identified what you need – let's begin with the end in mind and assume that your physiological, safety, belonging and esteem needs are fulfilled. Below is a list of characteristics and behavior traits of self actualized people as identified by Maslow.

Characteristics of self-actualizers	Behavior leading to self-actualization
1. They perceive reality efficiently and can tolerate uncertainty	Experiencing life like a child, with full absorption and concentration
2. Accept themselves and others for what they are	
3. Spontaneous in thought and action	Trying new things instead of sticking to safe paths
4. Problem-centered (not self-centered)	
5. Unusual sense of humor	Listening to your own feelings in evaluating experiences instead of the voice of tradition, authority or the majority
6. Able to look at life objectively	
7. Highly creative	
8. Resistant to enculturation, but not purposely unconventional	Avoiding pretense ('game playing') and being honest
9. Concerned for the welfare of humanity	
10. Capable of deep appreciation of basic life-experience	Being prepared to be unpopular if your views do not coincide with those of the majority
11. Establish deep satisfying interpersonal relationships with a few people	Taking responsibility and working hard
12. Peak experiences	
13. Need for privacy	
14. Democratic attitudes	Trying to identify your defenses and having the courage to give them up
15. Strong moral/ethical standards	

It is my goal to help you reach your potential. All self actualizing people embrace their potential, commit to something greater than themselves and passionately pursue a vocation or cause. Take a moment and think about your cause, vocation or something you would do even if you received no compensation.

Dig down deep and give yourself permission to claim what is in your heart. Use this time to fully embrace that which you have thought about being, doing or having many times. If for some reason you find yourself lost for words – draw a picture. Or better yet draw a symbol that captures your feelings. Let your heart speak and listen. Record what it says and don't you dare let your mind say it isn't so.

EXERCISE – VOCATION/CAUSE

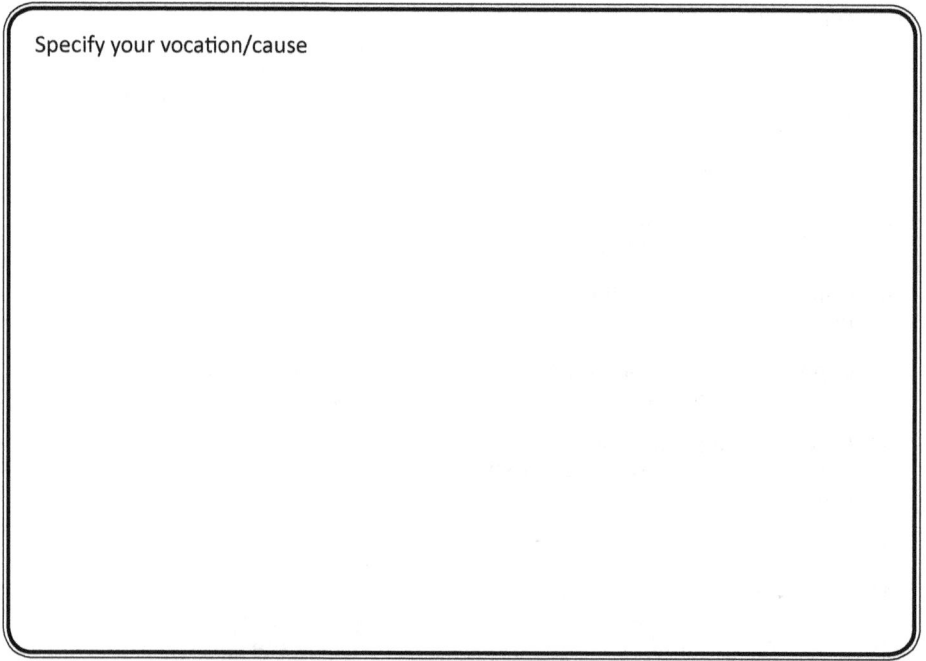

Specify your vocation/cause

Above all you must be willing to grow for personal growth is a fundamental element of self actualized vocation driven people. It will require courage and hard work to reach your true potential. Once you become truly committed to this cause, the necessary resources will appear. You will find yourself happier and more productive than ever before.

"If you plan on being anything less than you are capable of being, you will probably be unhappy all of the days of your life."
Abraham Maslow

If you have not committed to a vocation or are unable to claim a cause – do not fret. Keep reading.

A few years ago, Rick Warren's book, *The Purpose Driven Life*, appeared on The New York Times best-seller list. I, like millions of other people, purchased the book. Initially, I thought the book would help me figure out my purpose. My take away from reading the book was at the end of the day – we are here to make a difference in the lives of others. When we use our gifts and talents to help other people we pursue our purpose for being here.

If you are still not sure of your purpose, get a blank sheet of paper, free your mind and begin to jot down things you like to do. You may also use the computer to do this exercise. Keep listing things you like to do; when you get to the one that makes you cry – that, my friend, is your purpose.

Whatever it is that you truly enjoy doing or whatever it is that you want to be or become - claim it! For me, my goal is to become an Oscar winner. Each day and as many times as I can remember during the day, I affirm the fact or I say to myself that I am an Oscar winner. I even go as far as seeing myself walking the red carpet. I envision myself delivering an acceptance speech holding an Oscar in my hand. What about you? What are you seeing yourself do?

A secret to manifesting your ideal successful life is not only seeing yourself doing what you were called to do but hold onto the feeling that you experience when you think about it. Let the feeling eminate from you as often as possible. Also, consider creating a vision board. Cut pictures out from magazines that speak to your future. Glue the pictures on a poster board. On my vision board, I put my picture on Halle Berry's body along with an Oscar.

Recently, I got the notion to work for Tyler Perry. One day I drove up to his studios. I got a good picture of the studio in my head. Everyday, I imagined myself driving up to the gate and seeing the gate lift as I drove my car through. I reflected upon how good it felt to drive through the gates. Low and behold, I was selected as an extra to appear in one of his movies and a few sitcom segments.

EXERCISE- ATTEMPT TO ACCOMPLISH

What would you attempt to accomplish if you knew you couldn't fail?

---

1. Maslow | Hierarchy of Needs. Mcleod, S.A. (2007). Simply Psychology. Retrieved 4 November 2011, from http://www.simplypsychology.org/maslow.html

*"When you see the invisible
you can do the impossible."*

ORAL ROBERTS

CHAPTER 3

THE DASH

"There'll be two dates on your tombstone and all your friends will read 'em but all that's gonna matter is that little dash between 'em."

– Kevin Welch

The beautiful aspect of life is that as long as you are living you have an opportunity to work on how you want to be remembered. Students pursuing their Masters in Business Administration at the University of Georgia are required to write their obituary during the first week of a leadership course. Indulge me for a few minutes and take a shot at writing yours. You can state anything you want – after all it's your life.

EXERCISE – MY OBITUARY

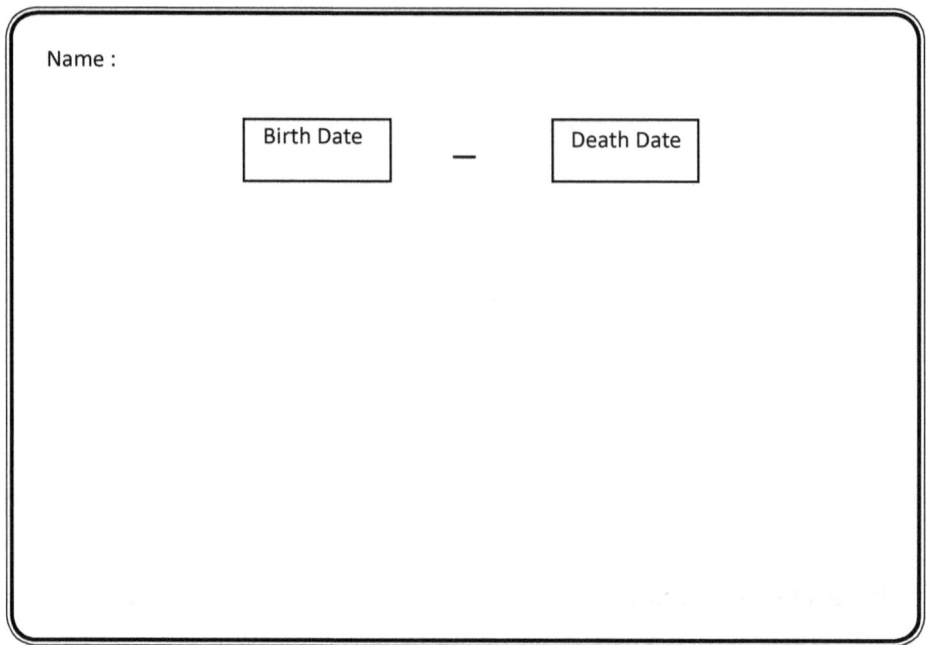

It's amazing how when we leave this earth, someone will have to pull together information concerning what we have done in our lifetime. But what is more amazing, is that today you can change what will be written about you when your body leaves this earth.

If for some reason you struggled with the obituary exercise don't fret. Keep reading and keep working the exercises as I promise-you will claim something extraordinary for your life.

Did you allow yourself to acknowledge something out of the ordinary? If not, why? If what you claimed does not stretch you then your aim is too low. Born in slavery, Dr. Benjamin E. Mays, President Emeritus of Morehouse College, ended up becoming one of the greatest educators of his time. He left such an indelible mark on the world that we still learn from him today.

Here are two of his quotes that resonate with me and seem befitting for this time and space.

"Not failure, but low aim is a sin."

"It is a disgrace not reach the stars, but it is a disgrace to have no starts to reach for."

With that said, how high did you aim? Was your obituary reflective of someone who left a mark on the earth that cannot be erased? Did it speak to someone who left a lasting legacy? Many times we rule out certain things because we feel like we have to know how we will accomplish our desires.

The real thing that we need to know is why we want to do something and if that why is for the greater good of humanity. If that why is not solely about you having or getting something but how you can help someone else then you can rest assure that the resources you need will appear.

When Harriett Tubman made a decision, she did not know that people who looked like the people committing the offense would help. All she knew was slavery was wrong, and she had a choice to stay or escape. She was very clear about the fact that she could change her living situation.

Indulge me for a moment and refer back to the Serenity Prayer. God gave Tubman the serenity to know that she could not change the people who had her in bondage. He gave her the wisdom to know that she could leave, along with the courage to do it.

Practically everyone in her predicament could not fathom the idea or the fact that they did not have to live as a slave. But she could and she did. And if she was asked, what would you attempt to accomplish if you knew you couldn't fail – she would say, "Rescue my people."

By now, it is my expectation that you believe it is always easier said than done. And friend, it is. So what is it that makes some people pursue what might seem like the impossible?

I am reminded of a speech that Dr. Martin Luther King Jr. made June 1963 when he advised the audience to, "…develop inner conviction because there are some things so dear, some things so precious, some things so eternally true, that they are worth dying for." Take a look at one of the more cited quotes from that speech.

> *"If a man hasn't discovered something that*
> *he will die for he isn't fit to live."*
> *Martin Luther King, Jr.*

Would you say Harriet Tubman discovered that which she was willing to die for? There was a bounty on her dead or alive for $40,000 back in the 1800s. But she is credited with ushering more than 300 slaves to freedom.

It is not my intent to give you a history lesson. However, we can always learn valuable lessons from people dead and alive. From Harriet Tubman's life we learn that there will always be a star to guide you. People will come to your aid. Resources will appear once you make a decision to keep moving towards helping others. And if we dare decide to die for what we believe in our life takes on a whole new meaning. Basically, we take part in something much bigger than ourselves; something that serves the greater good of humanity.

Have you found something that you would die for? I know it's a hard question. In pondering the question, my son came to mind. Without hesitation I would lay down my life for him. If you're a parent, I'm willing to bet that you would be willing to do the same. Aside from your children, if you have any - is there anything else that you are willing to die for? Or is there anything that you really, really want more than anything in the whole wide world to see happen in your life? Better yet, is there something that you are just dying to do? Let's take it a step further, is there something that you secretly desire to be, do or have?

EXERCISE – MY WILLING TO DIE FOR LIST

Take a moment to jot down your thoughts. Allow yourself to be totally open and honest.

"Excuses are monuments of nothingness. They build bridges to nowhere. Those who use these tools of incompetence, seldom become anything but nothing at all."

AUTHOR UNKNOWN

CHAPTER

HEART VS. HEAD

"The human heart feels things the eyes cannot see, and knows what the mind cannot understand."

– Blaise Pascal

Many times we think ourselves out of what we feel in our heart concerning our lives. For instance, you might feel as though you can do such and such but you allow your mind to provide you with reasons why you can't do such and such. No matter how long you spend deliberating what you can and can't do – you will always find that the feeling to do a certain thing remains deep down in your heart.

No matter how hard you try, your heart will continue to speak to you. It will overpower your thoughts, yearning for the opportunity to express itself outwardly. The longer you ignore the voice of your heart, the more you will find yourself frustrated with yourself and your life.

Sometimes we use artificial substances to keep our mind from letting our heart be heard. Sometimes we let people in our lives talk us out of what is in our heart. Sometimes we let fear of the unknown stop us from following our heart. Whatever, the excuse may be, it must be eliminated.

By any means necessary we must acknowledge what we love to do and find a way to do it. If we're smart we will find a way to make a living doing it. Let's take a moment to explore what is in your heart.

EXERCISE - MY LOVE TO DO LIST

List three things that you love to do:

1. ....

2. ....

3. ....

Now that you have identified what you love to do – it's time to start doing it more. Did you notice how happy you felt just jotting down what you love to do? Imagine how your life would be if you could do what you love to do all the time.

There are plenty of people who do what they love to do every day of their lives. If they can do it, you can too. As with everything in life – there's good and bad. Ask any entrepreneur and they will tell you that they work hard but they love it! It will take hard work, tremendous sacrifices and innate talents to do what you love to do and make a living at it. But the happiness you will experience will make the work seem like play.

Were you able to identify three things you love to do? Out of the three things on your list, pick one thing that you could not live without doing.

EXERCISE – ONE THING YOU LOVE TO DO

Pick the favorite thing you love to do from your list of three

/. ....

Somehow, some way we always find a way to do what we were made to do. In many instances what we love to do comes so naturally to us that we take it for granted. Often times we fail to realize that what comes naturally to us is difficult for others.

Actually, that one thing that you acknowledged is your area of giftedness. Your goal should be to nurture your gift and share it with those who need it. And if you're really good – you'll get paid in the process.

When you hear the names Venus and Serena what do you associate with them? What about Michael Jordan and Tiger Woods? They are merely doing what they love to do. And you can too – with prayer and heeding to the following suggestions, you will be well on your way.

- Practice, Practice, Practice
- Designate a few hours at least three times a week to research your area of giftedness
- Join an applicable association
- Get a mentor
- Acquire business acumen

*Go to your bosom; knock there,
and ask your heart what it doth know…*

WILLIAM SHAKESPEARE

CHAPTER

SEEING THE INVISIBLE

"We are limited, not by our abilities, but by our vision."

Have you ever seen the old black and white movie The Miracle Worker? It is the life of Helen Keller. I am often reminded of her story because she could not see, speak or hear. But despite those odds she still managed to earn a Pulitzer Prize, receive the President's highest civilian honor: The Presidential Medal of Freedom and win an Oscar. If she was able to do all that she did despite all with which she had to contend with - what is stopping you?

Now that you have identified what you are truly capable of accomplishing – it's time to start seeing it manifest in the earth. Someone once asked Helen Keller who accomplished great things despite her limitations, what could be worse than not being able to see, hear or talk? She replied, "To be able to see but have no vision."

Basically, a vision is defined as an image of the future we seek to create. All great companies and individuals have taken the time to craft a vision statement. At the onset of the creation of Microsoft, their vision statement was, "A personal computer, in every home, running Microsoft software." Fast forward 30 some years – I'd say Microsoft got it right and used their vision statement to propel the company to greatness. Let's take a look at vision statements from other companies.

Organization	Vision
facebook	"Facebook's mission is to give people the power to share and make the world more open and connected."
Apple	"To make a contribution to the world by making tools for the mind that advance humankind."
Amazon	"Our vision is to be earth's most customer centric company; to build a place where people can come to find and discover anything they might want to buy online."

If creating vision statements work for companies, how about using it for yourself? Like you, your vision statement will change. But it is important to put a statement in writing that speaks to your future, as it will inspire you to do what is necessary to see it come to fruition.

Your vision statement is a statement that speaks to an aspirational image of the future that you aim to achieve. It is a way to focus your thoughts, energy, actions, behavior and decisions towards what you want your life to be and who you want to become as a person.

There is no best way to write a vision statement, but it should make sense to you, as you will use it to guide you everyday. It will also be a point of reference to help you clarify and pursue your life's purpose. Make sure your statement inspires enthusiasm, excellence and encourages commitment. A good vision statement is well articulated and easily understood. It should reflect your uniqueness as an individual and your unique talents and contribution to humanity.

How about creating your own personal vision statement?

Take a stab at writing your vision statement as if you had already attained what you desire. Use words such as "I am" and "I have" rather than "I will be" or "I will have."

EXERCISE – PERSONAL VISION STATEMENT

Making a commitment to memorizing your vision statement will help you stay focused on your purpose. Let your statement be a guide that lights the way for your path. Let the passion in your heart fuel your dreams to fruition. Whatever you have claimed thus far should come from your heart which is the rhythm and beat of your life.

Have you ever noticed that when you get excited your heart tends to beat a little faster? Have you noticed that when you are doing something that you enjoy you feel more alive? If your statement fails to bring a smile to your face, touch your heart, or inspire you, how will it drive you to inspire someone else?

CHAPTER

BEING A GIFT

*"What we are is God's gift to us.
What we become is our gift to God."*

– Eleanor Powell

If I brought you a gift and never gave it to you – it wouldn't be a gift, because a gift is not a gift unless it's given. You have been given the gift of life. You also have a special gift inside of you that when shared with others makes you and the receiver better.

The way you do what you do is unique to you. Your special eccentricities enable you to reach individuals like only you can. Your life experiences have molded you into the person you are today. Sharing with others what you have gone through to get where you are today is the ultimate priceless gift that God wants you to give.

As you tune your heart and mind towards pleasing God, you invariably make a decision to become great. All great people make things better for other people. If I asked you to identify someone great, who would you pick? I am willing to bet that they made or make life better for the people within their span of influence.

EXERCISE – SHARING MY GIFT

> How do you or could you use your gifts, talents and or abilities to make things better for others?

Focusing in on helping someone else sets you up to be helped. It is aligned with the principle of sowing and reaping. Whatever, you plant – that's what you reap. If you plant corn – you reap corn. If you plant watermelon seeds there is no way that roses will grow.

If you are holding on to any unforgiveness, resentment, malice, hatred or the like – know that it is not serving you to do so. Let it go. If you find yourself, thinking about any wrong doings towards anyone whatsoever, simply say to yourself: I will reap what I sow. Believe within your heart of hearts that you will not become the person you so desire if you hold onto and seek to do something to others that does not build them up or add value to their lives.

EXERCISE – FORGIVE

> Who do I need to forgive in order to grow?

Before we move on, by all means make sure that you forgive yourself too. All of us have done unspeakable things that we are not proud of. Please know that it is not your responsibility to punish yourself. Learn from your mistakes and try not to do it again.

If for some reason this exercise made you realize that you still harbor hurt feelings towards someone, take time to write them a letter expressing how they hurt you and what impact their actions have or had on your life. You don't have to mail the letter but just putting your feelings in writing will make you feel better.

"Our prime purpose in this life is to help others. And if you can't help them, at least don't hurt them."

DALAI LAMA

CHAPTER

BRAND YOURSELF

"Lead with your brand and let the compensation follow."

– Dan Schawbel

Knowing what you love to do is the beginning to branding yourself. More than likely what you love to do is something that you do very well. Your challenge is to master what you love to do and become known for doing it better than anyone else.

Does the name Nancy Green ring a bell? Probably not, but if I asked you, "Have you heard of Aunt Jemima?" your answer would be yes. At 56 years old Nancy Green was hired to promote a new product which was a ready mix self rising pancake flour at an exposition in Chicago. Green's job was to assume the Aunt Jemima, Big Mamma or Mammy persona while operating a pancake cooking display. Story has it people were lined up to taste her pancakes and to see her in action. At the end of the exposition she received a medal and certificate from the show officials based on her showmanship.

After the exposition she was offered a lifetime contract to assume the Aunt Jemima persona and promote the pancake mix, which she did thousands of times across the country until her death.

If a middle aged black woman born into slavery in the 1800s managed to get known for what she loved to do – why can't you?

If someone approached you with an opportunity to do what you do best which is the thing you love - would you be ready? Better yet, how would someone know about you? Nancy Green didn't have facebook, twitter or the internet to let others know about her. Word of mouth was how the two gentlemen with the pancake mix discovered Green. More than likely someone told someone who told someone about a lady named Nancy Green who could cook really well and had a talent for telling stories.

She was given an opportunity to do what she loved to do, and boy did she do it. She did it so well that it allowed her to not only improve the quality of her life but others as well. In the annals of history, Green was active in civil rights endeavors during her lifetime too.

You will always be given an opportunity to display your talent. But you must remember that the time when you need to be ready is not the time to get ready. Continuing to do what you love with excellence will put you in a position to shine when the opportunity presents itself.

When a company has a product to sell – they market it. The packaging along with the promise associated with the product makes up the brand. In 1997 Tom Peters a business management expert introduced the concept of personal branding. He suggested that individuals should seek to be the chief marketer of themselves.

Personal branding is the process of developing an identity and or an insigna that is created around your name or your career. You use this identity to express and communicate your skills, personality and values. The end goal is that the personal brand that you develop will build your reputation and help to grow your network while inspiring others to seek you out for your knowledge and expertise.

As an example, my name is Paula Palmer Green. I use my last name to articulate to others what I do, which is help people grow. In developing my brand – I use the color green, trees and leafs to futher communicate my brand identity.

You might be asking yourself, "How can I go about branding myself?" The very first step you must take is to be very clear about what you do best. If you are unsure – poll about three to five people who know you well. Ask them what do you do well?

EXERCISE-MY THINGS I DO WELL LIST

> Ask five people who know you to tell you what you do well.
>
> Person 1: _____
> Person 2: _____
> Person 3: _____
> Person 4: _____
> Person 5: _____

More than likely the answer will be similar. Now that you are sure of your "do well thing" – it's time to get know for it and get paid for doing it.

Your aspiration might not be to perform at Carnegie Hall, but you can be sure whatever you want to do, you must do it as often as you can. The following steps will help you do it better and put you in a position to be ready when the opportunity presents itself for you to get paid.

To help you in personal branding pursuit consider adhering to the following suggestions.

1. Spend a minimum of three hours a week researching your area of interest; read books and articles

2. Identify someone accomplished who is doing what you want to do, learn all you can about them and study how they present themselves

3. Get someone where you live who is doing what you desire to do to mentor you

4. Join the professional association for your desired field and volunteer for leadership opportunities

5. Acquire professional training and certification when applicable

6. Build and work your network

7. Look like you know what you profess to do

If you put into practice these simple suggestions – you will be well on your way to embracing your personal brand. Granted there are other things you need to do. So let us continue by starting with what you would say if you met someone and you wanted to let them know about your personal brand.

It is hoped that by now you are pretty clear about what it is you do very well. If the makers of a product only knew how well their product was and did not tell anyone else – how well would their sales be? Not very good - right? The same principle applies to you. If you want to get known for what you love to do – you must be able to clearly articulate what it is that you do and more importantly how what you do helps someone else.

Let's work on your personal brand statement. The following exercise will help you draft a succinct statement concerning what it is that you do.

EXERCISE – MY PERSONAL BRAND STATEMENT

Hello my name is:_____

I am _____

Insert what you are striving to become or what you want to be famous for doing

I can _____

Insert an adjective: i.e. help, show, teach, design etc.

You _____
_____

Specify how you can serve or add value to the person listening

Examples:

Hello my name is Natashia Lewis. I am a successful business owner. I can brand YOU so that you can make more money!

Hello my name is Mallorie Pirita. I am a grant writer. I can help YOU secure funding for your non-profit organization.

Hello my name is Paula Palmer Green. I am a Certified Life, Career and Image coach. I can help YOU grow so that you can follow your dream and make more green.

Congratulations on crafting your personal brand statement! You are well on your way to promoting yourself in a manner that makes others want to give you an opportunity to do what you do best. Transfer your statement to an index card and practice saying it while looking in the mirror at least three times a day.

LIST OF ITEMS TO USE TO PROMOTE YOUR BRAND

- Logo
- Professional business card
- Resume, cover letter, list of references
- Portfolio of certificates, awards, work samples (hard copy and online)
- Blog/Website
- Social media profiles: LinkedIn, Twitter, facebook:
- Presence on YouTube and or YouTube Channel
- Wardrobe w/basic elements
- Email address with your name or if you are in business an address associated with your website (word to the wise avoid at all cost using your work email address for personal purposes)

Promoting yourself as a brand occurs daily. Techonolgy plays a vital role as you communicate what you can do for others. Before you show up – you show up. With a computer, you can find out a great deal about a person. Have you googled yourself lately? If you haven't – please do so. You will be amazed at what you will discover.

If you use your smart phone to call someone, chances are their picture will appear on your screen. When looking for a job you have to create a profile online and use the social media sites to network to search people who can help you in your job search.

You are competing with people all over the world. In need of a logo, I let me fingers do the looking and was connected with someone in another country who gave me a better price than someone in my own neighborhood.

No longer can you afford not to be technologically savvy. Each day you put off learning how to become more proficient using technology, the more new things come on the scene that you need to learn. With the proper equipment at a nominal price, you can host your own radio program in the comfort of your own home. Millions of people are making money using the internet to share their voice, gifts and talents with others. Even young people are on the band wagon getting paid to endorse products. Whatever it is you want to know how to do – you can conduct an internet search and learn all you need to know.

Please promise yourself that you will embrace technology and learn how to use it effectively to tell others about yourself. In life, either you do it yourself or you pay someone to do it for you. Speaking from experience, if you don't have knowledge about a certain subject you will pay much more than you should.

CHAPTER

LOOKING THE PART

Clothes can suggest, persuade, connote, insinuate, or indeed lie, and apply subtle pressure while their wearer is speaking frankly and straightforwardly of other matters.

– Anne Hollander

People will judge you by the way you package yourself. Your clothing items and the way you wear them communicates a message to others. The challenge is to make sure that the message you want to communicate comes across loud and clear.

Celebrities and people, who can afford it, hire a stylist to help them with their clothing image. Until you can afford your own personal stylist, there are some things you can do to get two thumbs up when your red carpet moment occurs.

For me every day is a red carpet moment because I truly believe that you never get a second chance to make a good first impression. Can we work on helping you not need a second chance to make a good first impression?

EXERCISE – MY DESIRED IMAGE

> In 7 words or less explain the image you want to present

Now that we know what you want your image to communicate – let's make it happen. Whatever, it is that you want to do, knowing that you can do it is always the first step. If you had to pick a famous person who embodies the image you want to convey who would it be?

EXERCISE - FAMOUS PERSON

> The famous person who embodies the image I would like to communicate is: _____

To move closer to presenting your ideal image begin to cut pictures from magazines of that person and paste them to a board. You can also add pictures of models that embody your desired image. Basically, you are creating a vision board. Put your board in a place that you will see on a daily basis.

Keep in mind that your personal features do not dictate whether or not you have a great image. In other words, you do not have to have certain physical attributes in order to have a strong, appealing image. Above all you must love the skin that you are in and believe that you are beautiful while striving everyday to let your clothing speak a language of affluence.

Perhaps you are asking yourself, "How can I look affluent?" Trust me, you can do it, one day at a time by following some rules that have been around for centuries.

The number one rule to put into practice is to always wear the appropriate clothing for the occasion. For example, if you are going to a picnic, you should dress like people dress when they go to picnics. Shorts, tee shirts, casual clothes are always appropriate. The last thing you want to do is wear an outfit that you would wear to a club to a job interview.

Secondly, dress for the desired position, status or station in life that you are seeking. If you are seeking to become a manager in the corporate arena, then dress like managers in the corporate arena dress. People will begin to treat you accordingly and when a managerial position opens up – you will be given the opportunity to apply. Always remember that you have to look the part to get the part.

Thirdly, make sure your clothing items fit well and comfortably. The last thing you want to do is wear something that is too small or too big. When you are comfortable in your clothes and they fit well – you are able to focus on getting your point across without worrying about whether or not your clothes fit. Always remember that when you look good, you feel good, when you feel good, you play good, when you play good you get paid good.

If you decided to go to a bank to borrow money, how would you dress? Would you dress like a pauper? Or would you dress like you were worthy of a loan? More than likely you would wear something that spoke to the fact that you were a good investment. Your attire would communicate the message that you are more than capable to conduct business, follow your business plan and above all generate revenue to pay back your loan.

I am reminded of the movie Beauty Shop which featured Queen Latifah who plays the role of a hair stylist. She decided to open her own shop after getting feed up with her boss. She wore casual creative clothes in most of the scenes in the movie. There is a scene in the movie when she puts on a business suit, takes her business plan and heads to the bank for a loan. After meeting with the officer she gets the loan because she presented herself in a manner that spoke to her ability to handle business. Keep in mind that it does not matter what profession you choose, just know that there will always come a time when you have to impress someone to get what you want.

Another rule to follow when dressing with more affluence is to remember the military. Always strive to make sure that your clothes are wrinkle free, clean, shoes shined, hair groomed, buttons in intact, brass polished and body in shape. The goal is to present yourself in a manner that makes others want to salute you.

So let me reemphasize, above all love the skin that you are in. Love your body just the way it is. If you do not like it, change it; but in the meantime put your heart and soul into dressing it so that you garner the respect, position and influence you deserve.

With the Internet there is no excuse for not knowing what to do, wear or say in any given situation. With that said, you really should not have a problem wearing the proper attire for any occasion or dressing yourself for the role you seek to assume. When in doubt; whatever, it is -- let your fingers do the walking and conduct and internet search!

Is all of this sounding simple? Maybe, maybe not. I suppose if it were that simple everyone would always look fabulous; but you and I know that, that is simply not the case. To delve a little deeper, let us go back to the basics and cover some tried and tested principles for dressing more affluently.

10 PRINCIPLES FOR DRESSING MORE AFFLUENTLY

1. Start with good fitting foundations; bra & above all Spanx (especially for women)

2. Indentify the type of clothing line, clothing store or designer that best fits your body type

3. Invest in classic/timeless clothing items

4. Put on a well tailored jacket when you need more authority and credibility

5. Wear solid colors

6. Use colors to accentuate and deemphasize your figure assets and challenges: darker colors minimize, lighter colors emphasize

7. Opt for quality versus quantity; well made clothing items will fit better and last longer

8. Use accessories to express your individuality

9. Avoid wearing the same thing, the same way twice

10. Adopt a signature item/piece i.e. bracelet, pearls, bow tie, stylish watch

Whatever is going on with you on the inside will show on the outside. How you feel about yourself is obvious to the world. Until you come to grips with your inner challenges of low self esteem, lack of confidence, low self worth and negative thinking, it is imperative that you take extra care to insure that your image speaks to the contrary.

On a daily basis strive to be the best you that you can be. Take the extra time you need to look the best you can by simply getting up earlier. Let your clothing selection match up with something similar to what your favorite famous person whom you identified earlier would wear.

When in doubt, know that less is always best. Simple understated clothing allows you to be the center of attraction. With the focus on you instead of your clothes – you are more likely to be heard.

Going forward – make sure that you possess basic clothing items. By doing so, you will project the right image at the right time. Take time to clean out your closet. Make sure you have the items on the following basic clothing item list. And make sure they are in good condition, fit well and make you feel so good that you want to dance when you put them on. If not, go shopping.

Have you ever found yourself with a closet full of clothes and nothing to wear? By having the basic clothing items you will be able to mix and match pieces to create different looks. The compliments that you will receive will encourage you to remember to stay true to the K.I.S.S. principle: Keep it simple student!

Women	Men
1. Black Dress	1. Dark Suit
2. 3 Piece Suit in solid dark color (jacket, skirt, pants)	2. White dress shirt
3. Crisp White Shirt	3. Dark jeans
4. Jeans	4. Khaki pants
5. 2 tops (one sleeveless & one long sleeves; black & your favorite color)	5. 2 colorful polo shirts
6. 1 Colorful Pashima Shawl	6. Tee Shirt
7. 1 Sweater/Shawl	7. Trench Coat
8. Trench Coat	8. Blazer
9. Footwear: flats, boots, pump	9. Footwear: black dress shoes, boots & sneakers
10. Great Accessories: Large Stylish Handbag, Necklace, earrings	10. Accessories: tie, belt, watch, bag to carry books, etc.

Now that you have a handle on the clothing aspect of your image – let's take a look at your finishing touches which includes your hair, skin, smile and make-up. Always, always, always get a professional opinion. My mother always used to say, "Other people see you better than you see yourself."

Your hair is your crowning glory. Make sure that you get a good cut, use good products and buy good hair if it will make you feel better about yourself. Whatever style you decide on, make sure it fits your face and is in keeping with the powerful persona you seek to present to the world.

Take good care of yourself. Eat right, exercise, schedule regular screenings and check-ups. Cleanse tone and moisturize your face daily. Brush and floss your teeth, get them whiten for if you take care of them – they will be with you for the rest of your life.

Visit a make-up counter to learn how to properly apply the right shades for your face and lifestyle.

Looking good is hard work. It has been said that beauty doesn't cost – it pays. Each day you get another opportunity to look better than you did the previous day. Take the extra time to get your look right, for doing so will result in your feeling better about yourself. And remember: when you feel good, you look good, when you look good, you play good, when you play good, you get paid good.

Bottom line – love the skin that you are in. Take good care of yourself and your clothing items. Make friends with someone who knows the art of style, as they will be able to help you perfect and present a more polished image. Follow the lead of the person whose style you admire the most and take clues from your favorite news-anchor.

On this _____ day of _____ 20_____

I_____promise to do my very best to look
    print your name here

my very best, every single day for the rest of my life.

_____
                signature

CHAPTER

HEED & HEARD

Write to be understood, speak to be heard, read to grow."

— Lawrence Clark Powell

You have a beautiful voice and it deserves to be heard. I am not solely referring to whether or not you have the gift to sing. What I am referring to is what you have to say to make the world a better place.

As you grab a hold of the notion that you can be whoever you imagine yourself to be, learning to communicate more effectively will enable you to move closer to manifesting the desires of your heart.

Exactly what are the desires of your heart? If you knew that someone could grant your every wish, what would you wish for?

EXERCISE: MY DESIRE, WISH, WANT NEED LIST

> I desire, wish want, need got to have the following:

I wished I could see your list to find out if it consisted of things or opportunities. Things come and go and for the most part satisfy us temporarily. Opportunities on the other hand enable us to do something bigger than ourselves. More than likely, the something is associated with helping someone else. We don't necessarily have to prepare for things, but we do for opportunities. When an opportunity presents itself, we must be ready because the time to be ready is not the time to get ready.

If someone approached you with an opportunity to do something that you have been longing to do, what would you say or what would you write to convince them that you deserve the opportunity? Or better yet, how would you say or how would you write something to let the decision maker know that you are the right person?

Your ability to effectively communicate your desires will serve you well. It will allow you to influence, inspire, inform and educate others. As with everything in life, there is a formula for speaking and writing well.

As you move closer to getting paid to do what you love to do – it is necessary that you let other people know succinctly what you can do. You must seek out opportunities to address groups, organizations, clubs and the like. If you are not sure who to contact or the name of groups in your area – conduct an internet search by starting with civic organizations.

Having a prepared pitch is a sure fire way to ensure that your voice is heard when addressing such groups. Four simple steps will keep you on track as you prepare your presentation. It will make your audience comfortable and secure because they will know where you are headed. And it will help keep you focused as you make your presentation.

Basically, a presentation has four major sections —the attention grabber, the opener, the middle, and the close. The attention grabber grabs your audience' attention and more than likely solves or addresses a problem or meets a need.

The opener is where you, tell your audience what you're going to tell them. The middle part, often called the body of the speech, is where you actually "tell them." This is where you get your message across. The close is where you summarize what you told them you were going to tell them.

STEPS TO A PERFECT ON PITCH PRESENTATION

1. Captivate the listeners' attention

2. Tell the listener what you are going to tell them

3. Tell them

4. Tell them what you told them you were going to tell them

STEP 1 – CAPTIVATE THE LISTENERS' ATTENTION

The first few words you utter will set the tone for your entire presentation. Most all public speaking coaches stress the importance of captivating the listener's attention. Listeners want to know what is in it for them. You must get your listener's attention immediately. A tried and true way to do so is to ask a question.

I'm sure you have heard radio and television advertisements that start off by asking a question. For example, would you like to be broke or rich? How long would you like your hair to grow? How much weight would you like to lose?

When you are faced with having to address an audience, make sure you start off by asking a question in line with the service you can deliver. A secret sales technique is to ask a question that a person cannot give you a yes or no answer. Notice that the examples above did not allow the listener to give you a yes or no answer. The questions made the listener make a selection between one choice or the other.

Other ways to captivate your listener is to state an appropriate quote, a short list of facts or figures or present a challenge or call to action.

Example: How important is it for you to follow your dreams?

"Dreams don't die, people stop dreaming."

How bad do you want to make money doing what you love to do?

STEP 2 – TELL THEM WHAT YOU ARE GOING TO TELL THEM –

THE OPENING

In one sentence or less state exactly what you are going to talk about. Get to the point. Do not beat around the bush. The last thing you want to do is waste a person's time.

Example: I would like to share with you three things that you can do to make your dream come true.

STEP 3 – TELL THEM -- THE MIDDLE

This is where you provide the meat of your information. For some reason, the use of three points, examples, words, or ideas is more memorable than if you use just two or if you use four or more. It may have something to do with the sound or the rhythm of a series of three: morning, noon, night; beginning, middle, end; healthy, wealthy, and wise.

Depending on the allotted time – you can elaborate on your three main points by providing facts to back up your statements and or claim.

Example: The first thing you need to do to make sure your dream comes true is to believe that it will come true. If you don't believe it -- nobody else will. Secondly, you must create a written goal with deadlines for a dream is just a goal with a deadline. Last but not least, you should use your written goal document and do something every day to see your dream come true. Remember, people don't plan on failing – they simply fail to follow their written plan.

STEP 4 – TELL THEM WHAT YOU TOLD THEM YOU WERE GOING TO TELL THEM – THE CLOSE

When you reach the end of your presentation, you must let your listener know by saying: in closing. When they hear those two words they will be even more attentive to what you have to say. After you have said in closing, tell them what you told them you were going to tell them. Restate your three main points and give them an opportunity to ask questions. Pass out business cards and get as many contacts as you can.

Example: In closing, I told you how to make your dream come true. I talked about how you must believe in your dream, the importance of developing goals to attain your dream. And last but not least, I discussed how you must follow your plan on a daily basis to see your dream come true. Are there any questions? If not, I would like to exchange business cards. Thank You!

EXERCISE – THE PERFECT PITCH PRESENTATION

What problem are you preparing yourself to solve for others?

Specify your catchy opening/attention grabber

_____

List three benefits for engaging your service.

Closing:

Example:

How would you like to have more time and money to spend with and on your family? I am a chef who specializes in home cooked meals for the average working family. I would like to share with you three ways I can save you time and money.

I can:

1. Save you time because you don't have to shop for food or cook

2. Prepare a delicious meal that your family will rush to the dinner table to eat together

3. Save you money because I purchase food in bulk at a discount and pass the savings onto you

In closing, if you want to spend more time with your family -- hire me I'll not only tantalize your family's taste buds, I'll save you time and money too!

CHAPTER 10

YOUR WORDS — YOUR WORLD

Watch your thoughts, for they become words.
Watch your words, for they become actions.
Watch your actions, for they become habits.
Watch your habits, for they become character.
Watch your character, for it becomes your destiny.

Your words create your world. Say who you want to be. From this day forward make a vow to avoid any negative comments period. From this day forward make a vow to eliminate the need to say anything that is not positive. For as the saying goes, "You have what you say." What are you saying concerning you, your life, and your loved ones?

For whatever reason you elected to read this book, know that it is my intention to help you lead a more successful life. Research reveals that it takes twenty-one days to break a habit. Instead of saying that you are going to stop saying negative things for the rest of your life, try saying, "I'm not saying anything negative for the next 21 days, and I'm taking that *one day at a time.*"

Take a moment to jot down adjectives that describe how you would like to be. The operative word is like to be. Identifying how you would like to be is a viable step towards becoming who you want to be. Look within and do not be afraid to identify some pretty bold adjectives to describe the person you are in the process of becoming.

EXERCISE: I AM

List adjectives that describe how you would like to be
Example: I AM: *confident, competent, creative, beautiful, rich, smart, etc.*
1. _____
2. _____
3. _____
4. _____
5. _____
6. _____
7. _____
8. _____
9. _____
10. _____

As you can see there are only ten slots but if you have a need to write more – by all means, please do so. You have now identified the type of person you are in the process of becoming. I'm sure you would agree that you do have room for improvement. I'm sure you would agree that you are not the person you used to be. What is important is, you are not the person you are going to be or in the process of becoming.

> *"If you always do what you have always done –*
> *you will always get what you always got."*
> **Unknown**

If you want to receive something different – you must give something different. If you want different results in your life, you must do something different. The very first thing that you can do to start receiving different results in your life is to take control of your mind. In other words, control what you think by replacing your negative thoughts with positive ones.

It is amazing to discover that we truly have control over our thoughts. Whenever you find yourself thinking negative thoughts you simply replace each negative thought with a positive one. For instance, instead of thinking you are too old; think about the fact that you are wise. Conversely, instead of thinking you are too young; think you are a quick learner with a high energy level. Instead of thinking that half your life is over, think about the fact that the best part of your life is yet to come. If "not" precedes an adjective that you use to describe yourself simply remove the "not". So instead of saying I'm "not" smart, pretty, handsome, thin, qualified, capable, able – remove the not and say: I am smart, pretty, handsome, thin, qualified and capable.

It is said that the power of life and death is in the tongue meaning that our tongue merely mimics that which resides in our thoughts. What are you thinking about yourself?

EXERCISE – MY SELF OPINION

> Take a moment to be brutally honest. What do you think about yourself?

Are the words that you used positive or negative? Do your words speak life? Does your statement acknowledge negative character traits? For instance, in the past I had a tendency to procrastinate. The more I acknowledged that character trait, the more I procrastinated. Then I accepted the fact that "I control what I think." I refused to continue thinking of myself as a procrastinator. Whenever I found myself attaching the word procrastinator to my being, I simply supplanted that thought with the thought of my being a person who always does what she needs to do before it is due. And believe it or not, the positive thought propelled me to get some things done.

What about you? Where are you going? More importantly, what are you trying to accomplish? It is my belief that you truly desire to touch humanity and make a difference in the lives of others. When you look back on your life and the people with whom you shared it with , some are still around and some are not. Nevertheless, you are still here for a reason. Your gifts, your talents, and your abilities are meant to be shared with others and or to make life better for others. The sooner you embrace your positive nature, the sooner you can partake in living the life you imagined.

> *"Go confidently in the direction of your dreams.*
> *Live the life you imagined."*
> **Henry David Thoreau**

So far, we have taken a look at how you want to be and what you think of yourself. We have discussed the fact that you have power to change your thoughts. And you now know what to do to change your negative thinking. You are operating in a pretty powerful place when you begin to eliminate negative words from your mouth and negative thoughts from your mind. However, since it took you time to become the person you are today – it will take time to change. Be gentle with yourself. Believe in yourself and know that you know that you know that everything you need, when you need it, will be supplied to you.

EXERCISE - MY PERSONAL AFFIRMATION

I am_____

Use positive adjectives to describe yourself

I make a difference in the lives of others or make them feel better by:_____
_____
_____

State what you do – hone in on your talent/special gift

My life is: _____

Specify something spectacular concerning your life

Example:

I am healthy, wealthy and wise. I make a difference in the lives of others by conducting life changing workshops, writing inspirational literature and delivering one-on-one life coaching sessions. My life is a phenomenal gift from God that I use to help others live a happier more significant life.

EXERCISE – MY I AM DECLARATION

I am_____
Specify what you want to be or become

I_____
Indicate what you are willing to do to attain it

My_____
Specify when your desire will materialize

Example: I am an Oscar winner. I write a minimum of three hours a day. My writing will yield me an Oscar by January 2014.

Make a list of five things you need to do to become who you intend to be (Make sure you put a completion date beside your goal)

1._____

2._____

3._____

4._____

5._____

Rewrite your declaration in the space below:

It is important that you speak your heart's desires into existence. Commit your *I AM* statement to memory, then repeat it with conviction as many times as you can throughout the day. When people tug at you to do this or that make sure their request does not deter you from doing what you need to do to see your *I AM* statement materialize.

It is often said that people do not plan on failing in life – they simply fail to plan and follow their plan. I think you would agree that planning is important. But how you use your time is more important. You will never ever be able to get back your time. Value you time and on a consistent basis assess whether or not what you're doing adds or subtracts from you.

GOD'S MINUTE

I've only just a minute,
Only sixty seconds in it.
Forced upon me, can't refuse it,
Didn't seek it, didn't choose it,
But it's up to me to use it.
I must suffer if I lose it,
Give an account if I abuse it,
Just a tiny little minute,
But eternity is in it.

Dr. Benjamin E. Mays

CHAPTER

ENCOURAGE OTHERS AND EMPOWER YOURSELF

"Flatter me and I may not believe you. Criticize me and I may not like you. Ignore me and I may not forgive you. Encourage me and I will not forget you. Love me and I may be forced to love you."

– William Arthur Ward

Could you imagine a world without people? I'm sure there are people who have crossed your path or who are in your life who you would like to imagine away. It amazes me that the very people who we care not to deal with – need our attention all the more. It is said that the people who we think need love the least – need it the most. I don't know about you, but people who have a tendency to vex my spirit by not being pleasant, positive, professional, cooperative and considerate are the very people that I want to avoid.

Unfortunately, we are not always in a position to remove ourselves from their company. Sometimes we have to work with people who we do not necessarily like. Sometimes we live with people who we love but don't necessarily like how they act. The fact remains that the only person who we can change is ourselves.

We cannot change the person who we think needs to be changed. But we can change ourselves by the way we think about another person which will change our actions towards them. Do you generally see the glass half empty or half full? You can see the person as a problem child and allow their actions to affect your being. You can focus on their inadequacies and get stuck thinking about the things they do or have done. You can allow negative words about them and their actions to utter from your lips or you can accept the fact that they are not in this world to live up to your expectations. If you want to truly have an impact on someone else – set an example for them to follow.

> *"You must be the change you wish to see in the world."*
> *Mahatma Gandhi*

It is not easy to maintain your composure when someone has done you wrong, said something wrong or rubbed you the wrong way. But when you hold onto the fact that what goes around comes around in life, what you sow – you reap, you will find that you truly don't have time to waist being judgmental, angry, bothered or bewildered by the actions of another.

By simply altering your view point – you will obtain a vantage point when dealing with others. Basically, a person or people will always pose the problem and on the contrary they will always provide the solution to the problem. Keep in mind that sometimes the problems that you will face -- is the face you face whenever you look in the mirror.

Recently, while shopping at my favorite craft store I saw a middle-aged African-American lady who was completely bald. She captured my attention because a beautiful gold piece of art similar to a necklace adorned her head. I looked at her several times and was compelled to give her *a compliment.*

"Excuse me," I said: "You are so beautiful." She looked at me and gave me a big smile. She said, "Thank you It's a gift of cancer, when I lost my hair I decided that I did not want to wear wigs. I looked in the books and saw what the African women wore with bald heads and decided to do the same thing." At that moment she became even more beautiful than Beyoncé.

I told her again how much I admired her beauty and she said, "Thank you, you know my mother told me that one cannot give another a compliment without pulling the beauty from down inside them." Immediately, I reached over, gave her a hug. We went our separate ways but that moment in her presence truly impacted my life. At that moment, I saw her heart, her soul and felt her love for self and humanity. Did I remember to tell you that when she smiled – she did not have any front teeth?

> *"We are changed by the people we meet,*
> *the places we go and the books we read."*

I will always remember her because she made me feel good when she said, "one cannot give another person a compliment without pulling the beauty from down inside them." Her words encouraged me to continue to compliment others whether I know them or not. And you know what? At the time my words could have been just what she needed to hear. Moral of the story, whatever it is that you are going through, you can rest assure that when you take the focus off of your life, plight or fight and focus on someone else, you in turn will be lifted. You will be able to see your situation from another perspective. You will come to realize that it is not as bad as it seems. So with that said who are you encouraging? First of all, you must encourage yourself.

EXERCISE – SELF ENCOURAGEMENT

List three things you need to encourage yourself to do.

1._____
2._____
3._____

Now that you have identified what it is you need to be encouraged to do, create an affirmation. If you indicated that you need to be encouraged to lose weight, exercise or maybe go back to school. The affirmations you would create would be: I weight (state your desired weight), I enjoy exercising regularly; I am registered for school next quarter. Above all avoid saying I will do such and such.

Remember, an affirmation merely claims things that are not as if they were.

Do people gravitate towards you? If you are a person who people like to be around then you more than likely make others feel good about themselves. On the contrary – if you find yourself alone most of the time – perhaps people shun you because they do not feel good in your company.

My grandmother who is long gone was such an encourager. To this day I still hear her words of encouragement. It as if her voice is pushing me to my destiny. Years ago she told me that one day she might look up and see me on television. I think I have done my Nannie proud, as I have been on television and continue to prepare myself for when the opportunity presents itself again.

EXERCISE – TOP ENCOURAGER

> Who encourages you the most in your life?
> _____
> Why did you select this person?
> _____

The word encouragement comes from a combination of the prefix "en" which means "to put into" and the Latin word "cor" which means heart. Knowing what a big difference encouragement makes in your own life, what can you do to help others "to take heart" when challenging situations arise?

Become aware of what encourages you, and do those same things for others. Remember everyone has times when they could use some encouragement. Therefore, everyone is a candidate for being encouraged by you. If an encouraging thought comes to mind, share it. It may not have the same effect if you wait. Don't let procrastination hold you back; strive to encourage someone daily.

It really does not take a lot to be an encourager. A good place to start is with a smile. Say please, thank you and do what your Mom told you to do: if you don't have anything nice to say then don't say anything at all. There is so much power in your presence. It is amazing how much encouragement comes by you just being there for someone. The most powerful form of encouragement comes in the form of listening. You can encourage someone by simply listening to them. When you're with others, you're telling them that they're important. Remember to always be sincere and talk from your heart.

"You need to be aware of what others are doing, applaud their efforts, acknowledge their successes and encourage them in their pursuits. When we all help one another, everybody wins." Jim Stovall

WAYS TO ENCOURAGE OTHERS

- Always say: please and thank you

- Be interested rather than interesting. Take the focus off yourself and ask questions to let the other person talk

- Take the initiative to reach out to someone you know who has been disappointed or is going through a challenging time in their life

- Contact someone who has made a difference in your life and express your gratitude

- Express your appreciation to others for a job well done

- Acknowledge what others deem important i.e. birthdays, names of children, graduations etc.,

- Return the favor. If someone does something nice for you, a great way to show your appreciation is simply to return the favor

- Present someone with an unexpected gift at an unexpected time

- Offer a helping hand; don't wait for someone to ask

- Let others hear you praise them to others

- Celebrate yourself and the success of others

In addition to encouraging someone verbally, handwritten and e-mail notes or letters are also a great way to encourage someone. Actually, notes allow the person to keep and read your thoughts anytime they feel it is needed. Consider encouraging someone who gives you excellent service; write a letter of commendation to the person's boss. You will be surprised how well you will be received if you take the time to write a letter of appreciation to people at work, your apartment manager, your child's teacher or your mail carrier.

List at least three people you will commit to encouraging. Please be sure to specify how and when you will encourage them.

EXERCISE – WHO I WILL ENCOURAGE

	Who	How	When
1.			
2.			
3.			

"People don't care how much you know until they know you care."

JOHN C. MAXWELL

CHAPTER 12

LIVING MORE FULLY

"Don't ask yourself what the world needs. Ask yourself what makes you come alive and then go do that. Because what the world needs is people who have come alive."

– Dr. Howard Thurman

What do you want to do before you leave this earth? When conducting my workshops – I show scenes from movies to illustrate my point. Per chance, did you see the movie "The Bucket List," staring Morgan Freeman and Jack Nicholson? It is a great movie that illustrates the point that it's never too late to live life to its fullest. If you did not see the move – I suggest that you rent the video. Meanwhile, here's a synopsis.

Blue-collar mechanic Carter Chambers played by Freeman and billionaire hospital magnate Edward Cole played by Nicholson meet for the first time in the hospital after both have been diagnosed with cancer. They become friends as they undergo their respective treatments. Carter is a gifted amateur historian and family man who had wanted to become a history professor, but in his youth had to deal with poverty, racism and thus never rose above his job. Cole is a corporate tycoon, eccentric loner, four times divorced, who enjoys nothing more than tormenting his personal valet.

Both are diagnosed with a year or less to live. Carter begins writing a "bucket list," or things to do before "he kicks the bucket." After hearing he has less than a year to live, Carter balls it up and tosses it on the floor. Cole finds it among the items and reads it. Cole pushes Carter (by suggesting he add things like seeing the world, sky diving, "fun things," etc.), and promises to finance the trip.

The pair then begin an around-the-world vacation, embarking on race car driving, sky diving, climbing the Pyramids, and going on lion safari in Africa. Along the way they discuss faith and family, and learn from each other.

Carter relapses and is rushed back to the hospital. The cancer spreads to his brain. Cole, who is now in complete remission, visits him there, where they share a good laugh and Carter crosses off "laugh till I cry" and insists Cole finish the list without him. Carter then goes into surgery, but the procedure is unsuccessful and he dies on the table.

Cole goes on to live to 81 years of age.

HERE'S THE LIST OF ITEMS THAT COMPRISED THE LIST.

The "Bucket List"

1. Witness something truly majestic

2. Help a complete stranger for a common good

3. Laugh till I cry

4. Drive a Shelby Mustang

5. Kiss the most beautiful girl in the world

6. Get a tattoo

7. Skydiving

8. Visit Stonehenge

9. Spend a week at Louvre

10. See Rome

11. See the pyramids

12. Get back in touch (previously "Hunt the big cat")

Have you ever promised yourself you would do something you have never done? Well don't put it off any longer. I challenge you to make a list of your top 10 things you will do before you leave this earth.

> *"A dream is just a goal with a deadline."*
>
> NAPOLEON HILL

My Bucket List		
Things I will do – My goals/dreams/aspirations	Target Completion Date	Actual Completion Date
1.		
2.		
3.		
4.		
5.		
6.		
7.		
8.		
9.		
10.		

The only limit you have on what you can accomplish is the limit that you place there. When you look back on your life, I bet you can attest to the fact that when you make your mind up to do something you generally do.

A while back researchers conducted a study with fleas. Fleas are incredible jumpers. In fact, a flea can jump over 150 times its own size. If a man had the same strength, he could jump over 900 feet high. To put things in perspective, the Statue of Liberty is 305 feet high from base to the top of the torch. A flea can jump 30,000 times without taking a break.

The researcher placed some fleas in a jar with a lid on it. The fleas of course began to jump, repeatedly hitting the lid in their attempt to escape. After about 20 minutes, the fleas begin to learn that they could not escape and stop jumping as high as they did to begin with, to avoid smacking their head on the lid.

Once they became accustomed to the fact that they could not escape, the lid was removed and the fleas continued to jump at the same height, never escaping the jar. Since the fleas believed they could not escape the confines of the jar, they stop trying. Because of their experience with smacking their heads repeatedly, every time they tried to escape, they never even bother looking up to see that the lid was no longer there.

Do you live your life out like the fleas in the jar? Have you been conditioned to jump only so high? Have you hit your head up against life's situations so many times that you are tired of trying? Have you had the wind taken out of your sails through discouragement, ridicule, and failures?

My friend look up there is no lid on your life. Make a decision to jump higher, and simply do some of the things you have identified thus far.

CHAPTER 13

MAKING IT WORK TOGETHER

"It takes courage to grow up and become who you really are."

— E.E.cummings

You are never too old or too young to be what you could have been. Now is the time for you to embrace the life you have more fully. There is more to life than getting up, going to work, coming home, cooking dinner, watching television, going to bed and repeating the cycle.

You were designed with, for and on purpose. The two most important dates in your life are the day you were born and the day you embrace your purpose for being here. Taking the time to assess where you are and where you want to go is the first step to getting there.

When you grab a hold of a vision for your life – you will invariably strengthen the legacy you leave behind. Your purpose for being here has everything to do with service to others. Knowing who you are and what you do well will open up doors for you to help others.

There will be times when you can help others with your finances. But the joy you will receive by using your talents to help others is priceless. Your talent is what you were made to do. It is your purpose for being here. When you embrace it and do it as much as you can – you position yourself to reap financial benefits from doing so.

How you live your life will determine the quality of your life. You always have a choice; you can change or stay the same. If you continue to do the same old thing – you'll get the old same thing. Life will pass you by and before you know it, you'll be old wishing you could do life all over again. But you can't.

This is your life. I do not know your scene. But I do know there is a certain way to act. The way you present yourself has everything to do with the parts you get to play in life. Be willing to study so that the only person you are competing with is yourself.

Take these lessons to heart and pull the answers to the excerises from your heart. You must be before you do and do before you have something different. Don't be afraid to be more, to do more or have more than you can imagine now.

Your thoughts and your words play a vital role as you grow yourself. The result of you taking the time to identiy what you want is the first step to attaining it. Using your affirmations and statements on a daily basis will help you get what you want faster. And knowing how to package, present and pitch yourself is a sure fire way to be more successful.

> *"You were born with wings,*
> *Why prefer to crawl through life?"*
>
> RUMI

EPILOGUE

"The older I grow the more I listen to people who don't talk much."

Germain Glien

I am grateful to God for using me to give you what you need to grow at this point and time in your life. If you make God your leader and follow him as you apply what you have gleaned from this book, amazing things will take root and bloom in your life. You will begin to attract like minded people who really care about your well being. The resources you need to do what you want to do will appear. And unexpected doors will open that lead to places better than you could ever imagine.

You are on the verge of a serious transformation. You and your life have taken on a whole new meaning. With self discipline and an unquenchable thrist for knowledge you will begin to see the things that you claimed in this book come to fruition. Keeping your mind on what you want will serve you as you serve the world with your special gift.

No longer will you aimlessly pursue nothingness for you know that you will always reap what you sow in life. Seek to always sow seeds of righteous, encouragement and love that you give freely to others.

Plant these seeds in the heart's of others and you will never cease to be. I am holding up high intentions for you. I believe in you. And most of all I thank you for trusting me with your most precious commodity: TIME=LOVE!

www.ingramcontent.com/pod-product-compliance
Lightning Source LLC
Chambersburg PA
CBHW070133100426
42744CB00009B/1820